LEGENDS

OF THE

COMSTOCK
LODE

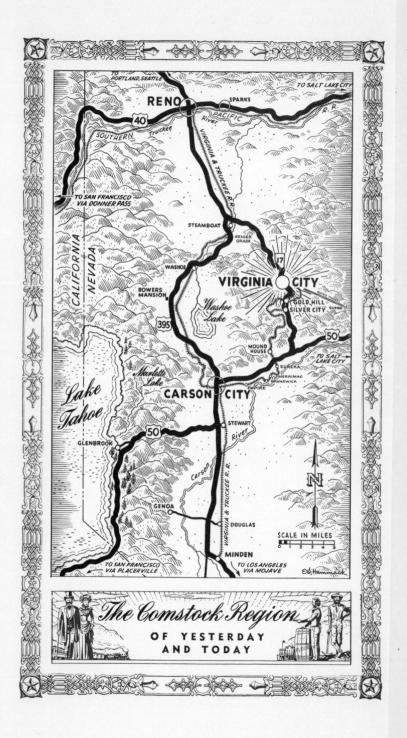

The Comstock Region
OF YESTERDAY
AND TODAY

LEGENDS

OF THE

COMSTOCK

LODE

by

Lucius Beebe

and

Charles Clegg

Decorations By

E. S. HAMMACK

Published By **GRAHAME H. HARDY** *Oakland California*

1950

CREDIT FOR PHOTOGRAPHS AND OTHER PICTURES IN THIS BOOK IS GRATEFULLY
ACKNOWLEDGED BY THE AUTHORS TO THE FOLLOWING INSTITUTIONS AND INDI-
VIDUALS: NEVADA HISTORICAL SOCIETY, ED ZIMMER, GUS BUNDY, THE BUCKET
OF BLOOD SALOON, GRAHAME HARDY COLLECTION, HUNTINGTON LIBRARY,
NEW YORK PUBLIC LIBRARY, HISTORY ROOM OF THE WELLS FARGO BANK &
UNION TRUST COMPANY, MACKAY SCHOOL OF MINES, NEVADA STATE HIGHWAY
DEPARTMENT, "THIS WEEK" MAGAZINE, ROBERT ALLEN COLLECTION, NEVADA
PHOTO SERVICE, C. R. BODEN COLLECTION, K. W. PENNINGTON, THE LIBRARY
OF CONGRESS, THE SUTRO LIBRARY, THE NEVADA STATE MUSEUM, THE CALI-
FORNIA HISTORICAL SOCIETY, THE BANCROFT LIBRARY, BOOK CLUB OF CALIFOR-
NIA, STANFORD UNIVERSITY LIBRARY, AND THE CALIFORNIA STATE LIBRARY.
THERE ARE ALSO CONTEMPORARY PHOTOGRAPHS BY THE AUTHORS OF THIS BOOK.

PRINTED BY

EL Camino PRESS

SALINAS, CALIFORNIA

In retelling these oft-told sagas of the Comstock Lode the authors are urgent to disclaim any new or original contribution to the literature of Virginia City or the legend of Nevada in its golden noontide of boom and bonanza. All the stories told here are available elsewhere in the not inconsiderable bibliography which has been evoked by the most glittering chapters of the Matter of Western America. These stories of the mines and the men who mined them are all in the record, but they are not, all of them at any rate, available to easy public access. Some are contained in one book of Nevada chronicles, some in another, and often the books are expensive or difficult of achievement by any but professional scholars or the most determined students of Western Americana.

It has, therefore, occurred to the narrators of these ten chapters out of the heroic past that a brief anthology of such matters might be of service to the interested public as well as to the fame of the region in which they had their origins. The wonderful legends of the Kaatskills have been assembled through the agency of Washington Irving so that every schoolboy knows about Brom Bones, Rip Van Winkle and the Headless Horseman of Sleepy Hollow. The ballad-lore of the Tennessee Mountains in its almost Elizabethan purity has engaged the attentions of a considerable body of scholars. There would seem to be no valid reason why the folklore of only yesterday on the Comstock should not, in what the authors of this book hope may be a popular manner, be also the subject of a book within general availability.

In the belief that the photographic camera is here to stay and that a picture is worth, not necessarily 10,000 words but is still of value, there has been included a variety of views of the Comstock, its characters and consequences both past and present. Where there are ruins they may not be of the nobility of those of ancient Rome or classic Greece, but the reader may be assured that only yesterday the premises they represent were the setting for a great deal of vitality, animation and hurrah. If he will consult the illustrations depicting some of the contemporary celebrities who make the Comstock their home or stamping ground, he will find that not all the names that make news disappeared from The Lode with the burning of the International Hotel. This is not a guide to the Comstock but it may provide some clues to the spirit of Nevada, both yesterday and today.

It is with a disclaimer to all but their retelling that we commend these legends to the reader to whom the American West must forever be the most compelling subject contained in the body of the national literature.

Virginia City
1950

LUCIUS BEEBE
CHARLES CLEGG

CONTENTS

I. How It All Began 9

II. The Legend of the Fair But Frail . . . 15

III. Money to Throw at the Birds 23

IV. Railroad to Golconda 29

V. The Big Bonanza 37

VI. Fleshpots 45

VII. The Muse Above the Mineshafts . . . 51

VIII. The Dream of Adolph Sutro 57

IX. Nabobs in Broadcloth 63

X. Sunset Over the Sierra 71

HOW IT ALL BEGAN

What was the Comstock Lode and how did it come into being?

The Comstock was the greatest bonanza in precious metals ever to be uncovered in modern times and probably in all history, although the wealth of Peru in the days of the Incas may have rivaled or surpassed it. The total wealth in gold of the Incas has never been definitively calculated, but the riches that poured out of the Comstock came close to the three quarters of a billion dollar mark. Two of its mines alone produced $190,000,000 in silver and gold in a space of a few years.

The Comstock, which was first known as the region of Washoe, embraces three communities, Silver City, Gold Hill and Virginia City, the last of which is located directly above its richest mines and is immeasurably the most famous. Virginia City, Queen of the Comstock, is built on the precipitous slope of Mount Davidson or Sun Mountain as it came later to be known, approximately eighteen miles south of the present city of Reno and in a mountain range which forms the eastern barrier of a pleasant series of Nevada lakes, valleys and meadows known as Washoe, Pleasant Valley and Eagle Valley.

For nearly half a century Virginia City and the Comstock Lode dominated the imagination of the world. They produced a generation of multimillionaires whose names are history and the saga of its fabulous bonanzas is an integral part of the mighty body of legend known as Western Americana.

Envision if you will the terrible and wonderful hills of Nevada, winter-bound and gale-swept six months of the year; reposing in the glare of a pitiless sun the rest, but holding locked in their bosom a secret treasure which was soon to raise empires and set the world's older treasuries tottering into the dust, was to finance the American Civil War and bring into being the city of San Francisco as the golden Carthage of the Western World.

Along the eastern slopes of Sun Mountain the fateful year of 1859 there might have been discovered a group of prospectors of far from prepossessing appearance or reassuring mode of existence. They lived in a tent town insecurely located on the east slopes of Sun Mountain and they were induced to a backbreaking existence in this remote and desolate midst by rumors, repeatedly circulated and sometimes doubtfully substantiated by sample ores, of a great bonanza in silver uncovered thereabout some years before by two brothers, John and Hoseah Grosch. But the secret had been lost with the death of both brothers and only a ragtag of prospectors, inspired more by shiftlessness to remain in the Washoe, as the region was known, than by diligence, continued to putter about Sun Mountain in search of samples rich enough to secure them a homeric drunk every Saturday night and a correspondingly stupendous hangover every Sunday morning.

Peter O'Reilly and Pat McLaughlin are generally credited with having uncovered the first significant silver ores in the Washoe. Actually they were prospecting for gold, and the heavy blue clays in which they discovered its traces were but a source of annoyance in the recovery of the precious metal. But one day in the autumn of '59 a specimen of the "blue stuff" found its way back to a sophisticated assayer in Grass Valley in the California Mother Lode and within a few hours the Western world was hysterical with the intelligence that the despised "blue stuff" was silver in unfamiliar geological form but of almost incredible richness.

The rush eastwards across the High Sierra was on and on a scale of concentration and hurrah which dwarfed to insignificance every aspect of the earlier California gold rush. Within

EARLY DAYS ON THE COMSTOCK LODE

The historic scene depicted above shows Henry Comstock, for whom the Lode was named, cutting himself in on the claims of McLaughlin and O'Reilly on the side of Sun Mountain in 1859. The character on the right may very well be "Old Virginny" who gave Virginia City its enduring name. Below is an exceedingly rare photograph taken early in the morning of July 4, 1862, in C Street at the site, a few years later, of Wells Fargo & Co.'s fine brick office. The Civil War was in progress and patriotism on the Comstock was at fever pitch to combat a subversive element of Southern sympathizers in Nevada.

a few weeks almost as many fortune hunters were hitting the trail for Washoe as had voyaged to California overland, via Cape Horn and the Isthmus of Panama in the first swaggering years of Mother Lode gold.

First to cut himself in on the Washoe bonanza was a sanctimonious gaffer named Henry Comstock. As soon as O'Reilly and McLaughlin had staked their claims approximately where Virginia City's C Street now runs, this prophetic fraud arrived smelling powerfully of Valley Tan, a potable essence of hellebore favored by the Mormon pioneers, and announced that Honest Pete and Stalwart Pat had jumped a claim to which he had previous and undisputed title. Comstock had the grand manner and for the occasion the grand manner was inspired to unprecedented heights by frequent reference to the bottle of Valley Tan in his coat skirt. Pat and Pete were impressed and dismayed. Working the claim of another man was a lapse in manners and etiquette in a community where these qualities were distinctly at a premium. Men had, in fact, been hanged for it. Pat and Pete were, therefore, overwhelmed when Comstock grandly allowed that he would permit them to work his claim on a percentage basis, and everyone headed for the nearest tent saloon to celebrate the partnership. Thus by virtual fraud and by fraudulant virtue of Valley Tan did the hitherto despised Washoe Diggings become the world-shaking Comstock Lode.

Next to take his cue from destiny and make an entrance on the now howling Sun Mountain scene was another boozy ancient named James Finney. Like Comstock, he was possessed of a sort of seedy grandeur and he was the lineal grandfather of all the whiskey advertising colonels who today sip their juleps in the coated paper periodicals amidst properties of the Old South. Finney was from Virginia and nobody within hearing was allowed to forget it, suh. He was widely and only slightly favorably known as "Old Virginny." One epic Saturday night when the camp was still young, while returning to his foxhole in the side of Sun Mountain Finney found himself taken in wine. Solicitous against the inevitable morning after, he purchased a bottle of Old Reprehensible and headed for home. But on the way catastrophe overtook the Old Dominion. There was a fearful crash in the night and then those within earshot heard the voice of Old Virginny raised in oratorical key. "I christen this God damned (and otherwise qualified) camp Virginia," screamed Finney into the darkness. He had dropped his precious bottle but he was going to have a christening party out of it if nothing more.

Virginia City had come into being on the Comstock Lode.

Twenty years later the mines of the Comstock had financed the Civil War; they had produced a crop of millionaires unparalleled in the previous history of the world and were on their way toward the billion dollar mark in silver production; they had caused Bismarck to order Germany off silver as a monetary basis and had reduced this once proud currency to the estate of a base metal throughout the world; they had established San Francisco as the most glittering and opulent city of the modern age, built railroads, the Atlantic cable and palaces in New York, London and Paris, and had elevated sourdoughs to the estate of bank presidents, ambassadors, newspaper publishers and tycoons and had married their children into the titles and aristocracies of the Old World. And Virginia City itself, a metropolis of 30,000 people, had become an integral portion of the American legend, a source of wealth and riches beside which the resources of the fabled mines of Solomon pale by comparison.

These were some of the forces set in motion by Peter O'Reilly and Pat McLaughlin whose source and origin will be forever the names of Henry Comstock, the humbug, and Old Virginny, the alcoholic orator.

Fantastically few of the original discoverers of the new El Dorado ever lived to profit from the incredible bonanza they had unearthed. Comstock himself, co-discoverer of everything in sight, accepted $11,000 for the fabulous Ophir Mine and a few years later, an untidy and garrulous gaffer, he made a noisy end of himself with a heavy bore revolver. While their claims, which they sold for $40,000, were producing a total wealth of $17,500,000 for their new owners, Pat McLaughlin was a $40 a month cook on a Montana sheep ranch and O'Reilly was dying in a madhouse, to be buried in a pauper's grave. Alvah Gould, co-discoverer of the great Gould & Curry mine, sold his share for $450 and spent it in the course of a single magnificent carouse in Gold Hill while telling all comers how he had trimmed some suckers. Old Virginny, who had named the queen city of the mighty Comstock, sold out for a quart of whiskey and a stone-blind mustang and he too was in a pauper's grave while a new generation of Comstock multimillionaires were swaggering through the bourses and money markets of the world. Alone of the first discoverers, Sandy Bowers, of whom there will be a more detailed report later in this volume, lived a few brief years with "money to throw at the birds" and a splendid mansion that is still one of the landmarks of Washoe Meadows down in the valley.

To the pioneers the Goddess of Fortune was as blind as the Goddess of Justice is supposed to be.

But on the heels of the tidings which were borne swiftly across the Sierra there came other men to the Comstock, men shrewder, more resolute and more sagacious. They bought out the pioneers for the proverbial song and remained to become the operators and beneficiaries of the seemingly inexhaustible wealth that had reposed unsuspected through the centuries in the depths of Sun Mountain. Their very names became legendary and Flood, Fair, Mackay, Sutro, O'Brien, Hearst, Mills, Sharon and Ralston will forever be part of the spacious saga of the American West.

THE LEGEND OF THE FAIR BUT FRAIL

The position of the madame in the nineteenth century American West might well be the subject of learned monograph or doctoral thesis were the tastes of scholarship in universities more robust and realistic. As much of a personage in any frontier community as the sheriff, the town banker, the Wells Fargo route agent or the parson, her personal character was as various as the personal character of humanity everywhere. Her archetype would be a completely worldly wise woman, far gone to be sure in moral obloquy and a shuddering and detestation to the respectable female element of the community, but proverbially generous, usually witty and the object of an affection among the menfolk that was about equally compounded of familiarity and chivalry. The rougher the frontier and the newer the outpost of civilization, the more exalted the estate of the pioneer madame. As urban civilization advanced and women of a "respectable" nature became more frequent to the scene, the lower became the madame's station in the social scale. But in the beginning she was half procuress and half amiable heroine to the frontier mind.

The Comstock's first and greatest madame, Julia Bulette, was the sublimation of all these things. One of the first two women to brave the rigors of Sun Mountain's shanty-town in 1860 — Eilley Orrum was there before her — she lived briefly and breathlessly to find herself the toast of the richest mining community on earth, the pride of the fire companies, a humane and compassionate strumpet who was tolerated by Father Manogue, and a Nevada notable who lived and died to become one of the imperishable legends of the Comstock Lode.

There are no extant photographs to tell posterity what Julia looked like, although a contemporary oil painting of a woman of undoubtedly voluptuous charms bears her name in a C Street saloon to this day, but she was undoubtedly Creole and there were visitors to the Comstock who seemed to remember seeing her in various mirrored establishments in New Orleans' Rampart Street in other years. A lone practitioner of the oldest of all professions in the Comstock's early days, she rose to occupy the exciting position of D Street's ranking madame with a rococo premises that was locally known, because of its comparative splendor in the midst of a growing mining community, as "Julia's Palace."

During the rough first years when women in Virginia City were numbered on the fingers of a single hand, Julia was noted for her domestic qualities as well as for her personal charms. When epidemics of what would today be known as influenza swept the camp she was a ministering angel among the stricken miners. Passing from tent to shack with what medicines the primitive resources of the community afforded she restored, among the ailing and even the dying, that hope which the mere presence of womanhood seemed capable of inspiring in the manly bosom of the frontier. When attack threatened by the hostile Piutes, it was for the protection of Julia that the men of Virginia rallied in arms and she was at all times the inspiration of their rough but undoubted chivalry.

Later when the mines began producing their fantastic riches and life became easier on the Comstock, Julia's Palace was the cultural center of the community. Only at her table were rough manners banished amidst the service of fine wines instead of whiskey and skillfully prepared French dishes instead of the beef and biscuits of the town's beaneries. She brought airs and graces where comparative barbarism had

"WAS THIS THE FACE . . ."

This putative likeness of Julia Bulette hangs today in the Bucket of Blood Saloon in Virginia City and is the only known likeness of the Comstock's most celebrated courtesan. Because it is unique and there exist no other portraits for comparison it is not an established certainty among students of Nevada legend if it is indeed she, but most agree it will do handsomely until another claimant may be discovered. It is the whim of its present owner to hang it juxtaposed by a deep red glass banquet lamp of the period much in vogue in Victorian times which is kept perpetually lighted in remembrance of the merry madame at whose dainty feet all Nevada once tossed its treasure and its heart. Below is the club car, "Julia Bulette," which once rolled over the now vanished iron of the Virginia & Truckee Railroad.

JULIA BULLETTE

reigned and the miners accorded her an homage that else-where would have been the prerogative of a great lady. The final accolade within their social gift was hers for the asking and she became an honorary member of Virginia Engine Company No. 1.

Now Julia set about expanding. Half a dozen of the most delectable articles in trade of the leading wholesale merchants of San Francisco were in constant rotation aboard Wells Fargo's stages over the King's Canyon grade. Their arrival and departure in frequent and provocative shifts and in fountains of ribbons and bonnets were viewed with unabashed approval by the masculine element of the community, but the ever-growing element of respectable women held up mitted hands in horror and daintily closed their ears with outraged forefingers at mention of Julia's name.

Julia, too, was becoming prosperous. When she took the air in the afternoon it was behind a matched pair of bays in a Brewster carriage imported across the Isthmus of Panama at great expense by one of her generous admirers. Another generous admirer had provided her with a sable scarf and muff in the latest fashion, by far the richest furs ever yet seen on the Comstock. When she occupied a special loge in Maguire's, screened from the general view but an object of universal interest, diamonds sparkled at her throat and ears. Wells Fargo brought vintage French champagne for her table, and cut flowers, the rarest of all articles of *grande lux* on the Comstock, were delivered to her door every day. The wives of the Comstock were not only morally outraged; they were consumed with embittered jealousy.

Julia's Palace might well have been called "Julia's bank," for her ever expanding business, which by the middle sixties showed tangibly in a neat row of white clapboard cottages with red lights over the door after dark, was making her wealthy even by Comstock standards and able in her own person to disdain the favors of any but the most agreeable and affluent customers.

Then one dark night something that the respectable married women of the Comstock were pleased to call retribution overtook Julia. Three men muffled in greatcoats against recognition knocked at Julia's door and were admitted, a circumstance which was afterward claimed to show they were known personally to the occupant of Julia's Palace. When they departed some hours later their arms were loaded with

"FOR THE RAPTURES AND ROSES OF VICE"

Virginia City's red-light district, known locally as Sporting Row (in other mining towns it was Virgin Street and Maiden Lane) was located on the west side of D Street. Some of these structures are still standing, untenated, alas, by the fair but frail who once were an integral part of any frontier community of consequence. Legalized commercial love stores disappeared from the Nevada picture, to the distress of many and the satisfaction of some, at the time of the Second World War.

furs and their pockets secreted a fortune in brooches, rings, necklaces, and gentlemen's gold watches which, in moments of insolvency, had been left as security in trade. The next morning Julia's French maid, prerequisite of all best pioneer madames, found her mistress strangled and quite dead in her elaborately ornamented bed.

There was hell to pay in Virginia City. The law was summoned. There was talk of vigilantes if the law was unavailing. The best saloons hung out mourning wreaths and the façade of Engine Company No. 1 was all contracted in one brow of black crepe woe.

And Julia had the finest funeral the Comstock had ever seen. Defying the domestic thunderbolts and what might prove to be the wrath of a just Heaven, the town's fire companies to a man donned their dress uniforms and assembled to march

behind the bier of the beloved fair but frail. The Brigade
Nevada Militia band was recruited for the occasion. A special
silver handled coffin was borne from St. Mary's, a concession
permitted by the Church because of Julia's notable charities
and good works, and reverently placed in the black plumed,
glass walled hearse which is visible to this day as one of the
sights of C Street. Then the cortege set out toward a hillside
a mile to the east of the town near where a later generation
of Comstockers would see rising the massive hoists of Adolph
Sutro's tunnel. Holy Church might be tolerant in the matter
of last rites for the dead, but burial within holy ground was
not to be considered, so Julia was laid away on a Nevada
hillside above what incalculable riches of precious metals only
the future might tell.

Then the band of the Brigade Nevada Militia marched
home playing "The Girl I Left Behind Me." It was a farewell worthy of an empress.

But even more cataclysmic excitements were in store as a
sort of legacy from Julia to her beloved Comstock. The mur-
derer, or what seemed to be a reasonable facsimile thereof,
was shortly apprehended. His name was John Millain and,
although he denied all knowledge of or implication in the
crime, he was found with some of the stolen goods in his
possession and, in its present temper, an accessory was as good
as a principal for Virginia City. A date was set for the most
stupendous hanging Nevada had ever experienced. A posse of
local architects assembled in the bar of Jacob Wimmer's Virginia Hotel to draw up plans and specifications for a scaffold
of esthetic design and regal dimensions. Committees were
appointed to have charge of routing the procession to the gal-
lows and other ceremonial matters.

The respectable women of Virginia City viewed Millain's
impending taking off with mixed emotions. By and large he
seemed an instrument of Providence for the ridding of the
community of its lady ambassador from hell, and Millain, in
chains in the sheriff's office, was fed, flattered and sentimen-
talized over in the best modern Sunday supplement fashion.

The day of the great hanging was a universal holiday.
Schools were let out. The mine hoists were silent. Gold Hill
and Silver City, their entire population on hand for the fes-
tivities, might have burned to the ground with no hand lifted
to sound the alarm or ply the pump. Even Virginia City's
saloons were closed so that barmen and swampers might

THE TOWN AS JULIA KNEW IT

Virginia in the sixties when Julia Bulette knew the town was
not yet known as "Virginia City." This came later at the fiat
of Wells Fargo whose executives liked their agencies to sound
important. It was a community of unpaved streets and pleasantly
roofed-over sidewalks with balconies overhead, a few of which
still cling to the façades of C Street to contribute to the old time
Western atmosphere of the liveliest of all ghost towns.

attend the ceremonies, and prudent and forethoughtful citizens provided themselves with bottles beforehand.

The hanging was a huge success. Flanked by a company of National Guard and riding in an open barouche from the town's best livery stable, the prisoner made a stylish arrival on the scene. He conferred briefly with two ghostly comforters from St. Mary's, thanked the good ladies of Virginia "in a ringing voice" for their favors of fried chicken, cupcakes and homemade preserves, and died in a manner which everyone agreed was most genteel.

Virginia City people to this day like to point to a spot on a hillside off to the east of town as the site of Julia Bulette's grave and at one time the Virginia & Truckee Railroad remembered her with a club car named for the queen of Comstock courtesans. The gravesite is open to dispute as there is no marker, and the V & T's club car has long since become a property of Paramount Pictures in Hollywood, but among the ancients who doze in the sun outside the first station opposite the Post Office in C Street her name is still currency and her memory, vicariously, green.

"My old woman's grandfather knew her," they will depose. "Said that Julie Bulette was quite a girl! Quite a girl!" Which may as well be her epitaph as any other.

"MONEY TO THROW AT THE BIRDS"

Perhaps because his mansion is still tangible and visible in
Washoe Meadows as a monument to departed greatness, perhaps because he was the first of the Comstock's millionaires,
and perhaps merely because he acted according to his natural
inclinations and had a good time with his money while he
and it lasted, Sandy Bowers is to this day one of the best
remembered figures of bonanza times, the archetype of all the
desert prospectors who struck it rich and cut a caper on the
strength of it.

Eilley Orrum, the future Mrs. Sandy Bowers, the future
Washoe Seeress, the future seeker after royal trophies in
Europe, came to Nevada from Salt Lake where she had dis-
carded two Mormon husbands, one of them a bishop of the
Church of Latter Day Saints. Her Scotch ancestry made her
a frugal and hard working woman and, in a region innocent
of almost all traces of domesticity, she was one of the first
women to hear the call of the Comstock and the very first
one to set up a boarding house there. She "did" for the
miners, washed their shirts, and spread a table which was celebrated all along the foothills of the Sierra for its biscuits,

beans and other substantial oddments dear to the pioneer digestive tract. With such abundant recommendations, she soon boasted the cream of the Comstock as her guests, "Old Pancake Comstock" himself, "Old Virginny" Finney, Pat McLaughlin, Pete O'Riley and Sandy Bowers.

Bowers was the shrewdest of all the original discoverers of the Comstock which, in the light of his later recorded sentiments and expenditures, may not have indicated an Aristotelian sagacity, but he had staked out a small footage in the very center of the lode and he stubbornly refused to part with it for the fleeting and trivial rewards which satisfied his associates. Precisely adjacent to Sandy's ten feet along the façade of what proved to be the United States Mint were ten identical feet owned by his landlady and laundress, the peerless Eilley Orrum. Whether it was that Eilley even then had a touch of the prescience she later claimed and took a quick peek at the future, or whether it was that Sandy wanted to insure his continued association with the only cook of consequence in Nevada Territory, Eilley and Sandy were shortly married and their claims on the Lode consolidated.

It wasn't such a consolidation as that of Gould & Curry or even Hale & Norcross, but it sufficed to make the Bowers the first millionaires of the bonanza and the first of the nabobs to inaugurate the expenditure of blizzards of currency which was later to be the hallmark of the Comstock success story. In almost no time the first of the stamp mills which were being set up down in Gold Hill was crushing Sandy's ore to the altogether enchanting tune of $100,000 a month, and Sandy and Eilley, whose rewards to date had been few and whose sacrifices many, lost no time in demonstrating that money talked, and with gratifying authority.

Innocent of the snobbishness and delusions of grandeur which prompted other Comstockers to seek homes on Nob Hill, in Fifth Avenue or the Rue Tilsit, Sandy and Eilley built a home as near the Comstock itself as was convenient, which happened to be down the hill in the pleasant valley called Washoe Meadows. When it was finished it was an amazement, even for its time, of gilt and plush, cloissonné, ormolu, pouffs, draperies and other bibelots dear to the Victorian heart. Their friends came down from Virginia City in droves and exclaimed out loud that surely no castle nor palace, royal lodge nor viceregal pavilion in all the world could hold a New Bedford spermaceti candle to it!

A PALACE FOR A QUEEN IN WASHOE MEADOWS

First of the great mansions to be erected with the wealth of the
Comstock in Nevada, San Francisco, London and Paris, and one
of the few surviving to this day is the home of Sandy Bowers
and Eilley Orrum in Washoe Meadows. Today it is a county
museum and memorial to the spacious days when Virginia City
swarmed with millionaires and no civilized portion of the globe
but felt the impact of Comstock riches.

THE FIRST COMSTOCK MILLIONAIRES

Sandy Bowers, a genial and illiterate prospector, and Eilley Orrum, otherwise known from her powers as a crystal gazer as "the Washoe Seeress," were the first authentically wealthy mine owners in the Nevada bonanza. Their grand tour of Europe, accomplished in a blizzard of currency, was one of the sensations of the sixties and their mansion in Washoe Meadows stands today as a monument to the expansive tastes and seemingly illimitable resources of early beneficiaries of the Comstock Lode.

The sentiment was not lost on Eilley. If this were indeed a palace then, as its occupant, she must be a queen and Eilley knew all about queens from the Old Country. They called on each other in the late afternoon and had a neighborly cup of tea while exchanging decorous but animated gossip about other queens and knowledgable royalties.

From that day forward nothing could shake Eilley from the satisfying belief that she and Victoria and the Empress Eugenie were indeed cousins, not even the expressed disbelief of the Lord Chamberlain at the Court of St. James or the indifference to her appeal to Charles Francis Adams, the American ambassador, whom history must forever record a churl for not, somehow, having gotten her at least to a garden party at Windsor.

Sandy was easily persuaded and a grand tour of the courts of Europe was shortly announced in the columns of the *Ter-*

ritorial Enterprise and other interested newspapers. Their departure was celebrated by a monster dinner at the International Hotel in C Street and Sandy's speech upon this wonderful occasion must remain through the centuries a model for frankness and good humor.

Eilley and he, Sandy announced from the fragile eminence of a French gilt chair, had known some interesting people in their time in and around Washoe, Horace Greeley and Governor Nye and old Chief Winnemucca. But now they aimed to see some even more interesting people like the Queen of England on her throne and this was by way of a farewell to their old friends in the diggings. Drink hearty, everyone, because he and Eilley had money to throw at the birds and wanted everyone to have a good time.

Tradition has it that all Virginia City had itself one hell of a time and that the International Hotel still showed traces of their appreciation a week later when Sandy and Eilley actually took off for San Francisco and the steamer to England.

The chilly Charles Francis Adams might prove impervious to the qualities and assets of the Bowers, but as much could not be said for the shopkeepers of Bond Street and the Rue de la Paix, nor even for the Muse of History. Denied access to the presence of Victoria the Good by reason of Eilley's unfortunate multiplicity of husbands, they were welcomed as only Yankee royalty could be welcomed to the ateliers of dressmakers, jewelers, furniture dealers and collectors of articles of what the age knew as *virtu*. The record shows them to have been the prize shoppers of the season of 1863-64 and during their stay in Paris alone their drafts against Wells Fargo back home came to more than a quarter of a million dollars. The Bowers had money to throw at the birds and the birds all wore frock coats and the reassuring manner of very upper class tradesmen.

Eilley and Sandy stayed in Europe and England for several years and their claims continued to produce fantastic sums of money to support their wildest whim and most expensive fancy. They called on Eilley's family in Scotland who plainly didn't believe a word either of them said and secretly harbored a suspicion that their Eilley had gone in for piracy on the high seas or, possibly, counterfeiting. Somehow — perhaps they were imposed upon, perhaps some generous person highly placed took pity on Eilley's pathetic hunger for royal properties — they obtained cuttings from the royal ivy which overgrows the walls of Windsor Castle and, armed with this symbol of success, the Bowers returned in triumph to the Comstock.

Several hundred thousand dollars worth of French mirrors, Italian statuary, bronzes, oil paintings, crystal chandeliers, Turkey carpets, morocco-bound volumes of the classics — although Sandy never could tell whether the text was upside down or not — marble fountains and suites of bedroom furniture came with them. But long after she had tired of these rich treasures, Eilley delighted to show visitors and especially friends who had known her in the lean years the cuttings from the Windsor Castle ivy now growing luxuriously over the massive walls of her Washoe mansion. A personal gift from Victoria to Eilley, a royal token of friendship from one reigning monarch to another Very Exalted Personage.

In time, in the late sixties, Sandy died and was buried in the hillside back of his splendid home in Washoe Meadows. The Bowers claims ran out and Eilley was reduced to taking in picnickers at the mansion for a living and a little crystal gazing on the side. Then after years of poverty, she joined Sandy in the shadow of the guardian Sierra and under the pine trees that whisper ceaselessly of the golden and irretrievable past. But the ivy from Windsor Castle, which Eilley had tried to destroy when they took her mansion away from her and sent her to the old ladies' home, grows strongly still, probably the only thing in Nevada which cherishes memories of two queens.

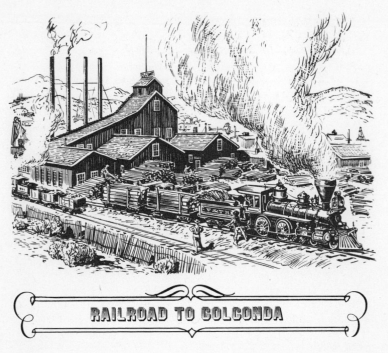

RAILROAD TO GOLCONDA

Beyond any doubt the one Comstock institution that functioned longer, achieved more enduring fame and whose name became more synonymous with Nevada than any other tangible asset except the Lode itself was the Virginia & Truckee Railroad. For more than eighty years of unbroken and useful service its operations were at first the wonder of the railroad world and later the most picturesque of working antiquities. Long after the mineshafts of Hale & Norcross and Consolidated Virginia that brought it into being were sealed forever and long after its builders, the mighty Darius Mills and shrewd William Sharon of the Bank of California, had routed their private cars for the last time over its circuitous rails, the V & T was a functioning Nevada tradition, a venerable gaffer among the railroads of the world. It had outlived its spendthrift youth and even its substantial maturity, but it still precariously rolled the mail, freight and a few passengers over its grass-grown right of way to become an imperishable actor in the great cavalcade of American railfaring.

Other railroads have had other terminals, but the V & T's generations of dispatchers now long dead gave it a green light and a clear track without slow orders and straight to immortality.

By the late sixties fortunes of the Comstock were, after a full decade of thundering production, operating in borrasca and the end of their yield was in sight. Because of the freight charges of the teamsters who hauled the ore down to the mills which lined the Carson River from Dayton to Empire only the richest ores were worth processing, and timber with which to shore up the deep stopes, drifts and winzes of the mines was equally prohibitively priced. Millions of dollars in inferior ores lay on the mine dumps below Virginia City and millions more were almost at hand below ground but was unavailable because of the excessive cost of getting at it.

The Bank of California's manager on the Comstock was a dapper and infinitely foresighted little man named William Sharon. Sharon knew that a railroad was what the doctor prescribed for the ailing Comstock. It would take the ore down to the mills at a fraction of the teamster's prices, thus making the inferior ores now above ground available to reduction, and it could bring up timber from the forests of the Sierra at fantastic savings to continue operation of the mines. But Sharon wasn't satisfied simply with the idea of building a railroad and taking a profit from its operations in freight and passengers. It might not be said that Sharon was greedy, but he had a remarkably acquisitive intelligence and so, with a grand over-all design in the back of his steel trap mind, he began allowing the mill owners of the Comstock to overextend themselves financially at his bank, took their paper when he knew it to be quite unsecured by any possibility of future earnings and kept the matter of the railroad under his well groomed silk top hat. When the mill owners were unable to meet their obligations and so were completely in the power of the Bank of California, Sharon coolly organized them in a single association, each member of which was obligated to patronize the railroad after it was built and otherwise do the bidding of the bank in every detail of its conduct.

Then and only then did Sharon build his railroad.

The V & T was originally planned to run only from the mineshafts on Sun Mountain down to the long array of stamping mills along Carson Water, but with the transcontinental railroad now passing through Reno only thirty odd miles away it was inevitable that the V & T should build from Carson to a Reno connection.

The first shovelful of earth was turned for the V & T's grade in the shadow of the mint at Carson City early on the morning of September 27, 1869, and from that moment down to the immediate present the V & T has participated almost daily, and often in matters of tumult and importance, in the news of Nevada. When, in 1875, the great stone shops and engine houses in the meadows outside Carson City were completed, a local notable named Colonel Curry conceived the idea of a monster railroad ball. For weeks all Nevada was in a tizzy of excitement and newspapers carried daily accounts of reports of the decorations committee, the decisions in the matter of refreshments and how the resourceful colonel was sending to far-off San Francisco for an orchestra at the unheard-of outlay of $500! When the ball itself took place special trains brought the elite of the Comstock down to Carson in their Paisley shawls and broadcloth tailcoats on special trains for the gala event and the last special didn't head up the grade with its cargo of wilted revelers next morning until nine o'clock. Nevada has never forgotten the great railroad ball of 1875.

Once in operation, the V & T surpassed the wildest dreams of its projectors. Not only did they own the railroad, but the nabobs of the Comstock were carrying aboard it their own ores to mills which they controlled and returning with lumber from forests they also had acquired. Only the cynical would call it a monopoly, but for many years Mills, Sharon and William Ralston, each a third owner of the V & T, divided $100,000 a month in profits from their railroad alone.

Unlike most men of property of a later generation, the owners of the V & T were proud of the appearance of their bonanza railroad and nothing was too good for it. The most powerful engines, the finest and most beautiful rolling stock in all the West made their first appearance on the V & T. Its locomotives were miracles of red paint and gold trim and its coaches were the products of the master car builders of San Francisco and the East. The V & T's owners had the idea, now quaint and outmoded in American finance, that a fine property deserved well at the hands of its proprietors and that they were under obligation, while pocketing gratifying sums from the V & T, to give the public something in return.

It was inevitable, with the wealth that was pouring from the mineshafts of Virginia City and Gold Hill promising to total a billion dollars, that notables from all over the world should want to see the source of these iridescent wonders. Metallurgists came from Germany, mine experts voyaged from distant Cornwall, the Baron Rothschild and his entourage (a whole special train for them) arrived from London and mere American millionaires, capitalists, stock promoters, newspaper reporters and magazine writers were a dime a dozen in C Street and the bar of the International Hotel.

They all came up over the V & T, in beautiful canary colored coaches, in overnight sleepers from San Francisco and Sacramento and in the clever Mr. Pullman's Palace Cars, each according to his station and means. President Grant, General Sherman, Helena Modjeska, Salvini Booth, MacCullough and David Belasco. Some of the maharajahs of super-finance came in private cars of fearful and wonderful design with vast resources of marble bathtubs, tufted satin boudoirs and brass bound observation platforms. It is hard, even to the enlightened fancy of a later generation, to imagine the V & T yards down the hill a pace from C Street alive of a morning with switch engines shifting traffic and the arriving hundreds of adventurers, business men and sightseers. But so it once was, and in the evening the light from the crystal chandeliers of stately private cars shone through the drawn silk shades, and women in evening gowns from Paris and New York tripped daintily up their carpeted steps for intimate suppers of quail and champagne. The years of the ortolans on the V & T were very, very splendid indeed.

When the long twilight of its career set in as the mines slowed and finally ceased altogether, the V & T shortly after the turn of the century, changed character from a bonanza railroad to one of rustic and agricultural destinies. It built the Minden branch tapping the rich dairy and ranching resources to the south of Carson City, and for a time the traffic in milk, butter, cheese and stock shored up its declining revenue. But the automobile and the speed highway which paralleled every mile of the railroad's main line abolished its passenger traffic except for occasional excursions and a few sentimental voyagers into the past and during the last few years the V & T depended almost entirely on the mail contract and a modest source of revenue from heavy freight shipped in on slow schedules.

For a time the railroad was the personal property of Ogden L. Mills, grandson of its original builder, who, a generous, sensible man, kept it running out of his private pocket.

CURTAINS FOR OLD 27

The V & T's locomotive No. 27 was retired in the summer of
1948 and here it is on its final run in regular service with a
mixed train emerging from the rocky confines of Washoe Canyon. After the retirement of No. 27 the road's two remaining
engines, Nos. 5 and 26, alternated in road service occasionally
running together as a double header when stock extras or
uncommonly heavy trains were scheduled.

THE GLORY OF THE RAILROAD IS DEPARTED

The Virginia City depot of the V & T was once a busy place as the trains for San Francisco and Reno arrived in the mornings and departed at dusk, but in 1950 only a hydrant stands in a vacant lot to show where once the Pullmans stood. The depot's site was between D and E streets where the V & T's yards included a freight shed, engine house and an elaborate trackage. The main line ran under "The Divide" in a series of tunnels and emerged at Gold Hill near where Grinder's Bend is today located.

VIGNETTES ON THE V & T

Up to the end the V & T was a silver railroad and shown above is a shipment of silver dollars from the Federal Reserve Bank in San Francisco being unloaded at Carson depot. Beside it is the old time lamp from the platform of the historic station at Carson City. Below is a double headed excursion train leaving the station at Gold Hill just before the line between Carson City and Virginia City was torn up in 1938.

No matter how lean the years upon which it had fallen, the V & T could glory in the circumstance, noted on its eightieth birthday, that it was the most celebrated short line railroad in the world.

"Just how colorful the legend of the V & T has come to be," said the *Nevada Appeal* in the fall of 1949, "is best illustrated by the fact that it figures in more literature than most main line railroads and that no other little railroad ever attracted a quarter the attention of the V & T in books and periodicals, monographs and histories both technical and popular, Bancroft, Eliot Lord, George Lyman, Dan DeQuille and Oscar Lewis are only a few of the writers who have been fascinated by one aspect or another of what Lucius Beebe and Charles Clegg in their *Mixed Train Daily* have called 'the Yankee Princess of bonanza railroads.' It is a certainty that the V & T will enjoy a fragrant immortality as the most literary of all the little feeder lines that once abated time and distance in the imperishable American West."

The original main line of the V & T between Carson and Virginia City was torn up in 1938, but sometimes on clear winter nights when the snow lies heavy on the slopes of Sun Mountain and the coyotes and prairie dogs hold carnival down Six Mile Canyon, old inhabitants of the Comstock hear a soft huff-puffing of wood burning engines and the clatter of couplings and they know, no matter what anyone else may say, that the Night Express for San Francisco is being made up in the yards and that the V & T is still carrying the old bearded Kings of the Comstock and their treasure down the grade to immortality.

THE BIG BONANZA

Bonanza is a Spanish mining word meaning solvent, profitable, in the money, or paying off. Its opposite, *borrasca*, just as common usage in the jargon of mining but less in popular circulation, means to be operating at a loss.

The phrase, "The Big Bonanza," usually capitalized to set it apart from all other discoveries of precious metals just as, in many communities "The Big Fire" sets some particularly notable holocaust apart from all others, is conventionally used in the lexicon of the Comstock to describe a single momentous uncovery of riches at a specific date and does not refer to the profitable working of the Comstock Lode as a whole.

The Big Bonanza, which was to produce one hundred and ninety million dollars in almost pure silver in a single block of precious metal, was to raise to almost unbelievable wealth an entire new dynasty of American millionaires and was to create panic, terror and disintegration on all the bourses, stock exchanges and money markets of the world, was the result of good fortune, great resolution, an uncommon knowledge of mining and an ability to keep a screaming secret on the part of four astute and determined men. James Flood,

James Fair, John Mackay and William S. O'Brien were no ignorant prospectors who stumbled by mischance upon fantastic wealth. They were extremely capable mine operators who were sure there was a tremendous bonanza awaiting the proper exploitation of their property and who clung to this belief against the better judgment of others until it was justified on a scale that made them the most envied men in the world.

By the year 1873 the mines of the Comstock had been in and out of bonanza half a dozen times. After each slump, new mining methods, enlarged facilities or renewed persistence upon the part of geologists and mine foremen had uncovered new treasure houses deep on the slopes of Sun Mountain. Blow hot, blow cold, Virginia City was always either on top of the world or in the lowest dumps of depression. The mines were played out, so the rumor ran, and the miners and prospectors were off bag and baggage to the newly reported strikes along the Reese River and in the White Pine district. The huge bonanza in Crown Point dispelled the gloom. The ores were getting so lean they weren't worth milling. The Virginia & Truckee Railroad disproved that fallacy and the goose hung high again.

By 1873 the Comstock had been through a dozen depressions, created scores of millionaires, was the occasion of a thousand suicides, and had alternately panicked and rejoiced the Mining Exchange down in San Francisco until hysteria seemed the normal aspect of life and sudden riches and sudden ruin the conventional order of things.

The partnership of Flood, Fair, Mackay and O'Brien had profited in a fairly substantial way from such mines as Kentuck and Hale & Norcross in which they had interested themselves. They were on the way to becoming men of substance, but that meant nothing in the dreams which haunted men on the Comstock, and besides they had lost heavily in prospecting the unprofitable Savage. Fair and Mackay worked as superintendents on the actual scene of operations in Virginia City while Flood and O'Brien, the former saloon keepers and contact men, represented their interests in San Francisco, watched the market and spread information which advanced or depressed stocks to the advantage of the partnership.

Mackay was obsessed with the belief that there was rich ore to be taken out of two despised and then comparatively worthless properties lying adjacent to each other in the middle of

THE WORKS OF THE GREAT YELLOW JACKET

In 1893 the shafts and hoists of the fabulous Yellow Jacket Mine dominated the town of Gold Hill and had contributed $20,000,000 to the total of Comstock wealth. Destroyed by a catastrophic fire some years previously, it had been reopened with the most modern pumps and other machinery whose intricacy and elaborate pattern are indicated by the photograph shown below.

VIRGINIA CITY IN THE GOLDEN YEARS

In 1880 Virginia City, Queen of the Comstock, boasted a permanent population of more than 25,000 persons and another 5,000 transients. Its International Hotel, in the precise center of this old time photograph, was an amazement of luxury apartments crowded with notables and set down in the middle of the Nevada desert. The great Con-Virginia and California mines, whose stacks appear to the right and behind the International, were producing a generation of millionaires whose wives were the prize customers in the Strand, the Rue de la Paix and Fifth Avenue. The fire of 1875 had rid the town of its shacks and hovels of early days and in their place were substantial dwellings, handsome brick business premises and the lordly mansions of mine owners and superintendents.

VIRGINIA CITY, THE LIVELY GHOST

Virginia City in the mid-nineteenth century seen from the identical spot as on the page opposite is no longer the howling wonder of the Western world, but it advertises itself with no small justification as "The Liveliest Ghost Town on Earth." In summer C Street swarms with tourists and seekers after historic atmosphere and the same remarkable music boxes that assaulted the ears of Jim Fair and Hank Monk sneeze and clatter in the Comstock's bewilderment of saloons, pool halls and curio shops. After the second World War Virginia began enjoying a boom of gratifying proportions. A luxury restaurant in the one-time King mansion in Howard Street and an authentic literary colony emerged upon the scene and new pleasure resorts bloomed in the center of town. The bonanza might not be of Gould & Curry proportions but Virginia City welcomed it none the less.

SOURCE AND FOUNTAINHEAD OF FORTUNE

The richest silver mine in the history of the world was Consolidated Virginia here shown in the days when it was producing $190,000,000 in precious metals for the bonanza kings, Flood, Fair, Mackay and O'Brien. One of the cars on the adjacent track of the V & T is the overnight Central Pacific sleeper from San Francisco. Below is the great pump of the neighboring Union Mine whose flywheel was an amazing thirty-six feet in diameter and was installed at a cost of more than half a million dollars. Machinery for the mines on the Comstock consumed a ponderable part of the profit from their operations.

the Comstock profile. Consolidated Virginia and California had produced nothing but assessments for their stockholders although they were strategically situated between the rich and prosperous properties of Ophir and Best & Belcher, but, at Mackay's word, Flood and Fair down in San Francisco began buying stock in California and Con Virginia at depressed rates on the San Francisco market and, when control of the property was assured, Mackay and Fair sank an exploratory shaft in Con Virginia, obtaining at the same time permission from the management of nearby Gould & Curry to join it with an exploratory drift from that mine's 1,100 foot level. Fair was below ground the day his workmen cut into an eighth of an inch of pure silver ore. Instantly he ordered the drift turned to follow this elusive seam. It ran briefly and disappeared, repeating the performance for several weeks until one day, well inside the bounds of Con Virginia it amazingly opened into a vein fully seven feet wide. The partners held their breath, both in C Street and down the hill in Montgomery Street. They held their counsel, too, and continued to buy up Con Virginia and California whenever a block of either stock appeared on the market. At the bottom of the shaft of Con Virginia a new drift was cut following the course of the one higher up and after tunneling less than 300 feet Fair and Mackay cut into a block of almost pure silver fifty-four feet wide and of as yet undetermined height and depth.

This was it. This was The Big Bonanza.

The assays, which ran as high as an unbelievable (considering the volume of ore in sight) $630 a ton, were kept secret. Con Virginia began producing immediately but not through its own shaft. That would have given the C Street tipsters a notion of what was toward. It was brought up in dead of night by trusted gangs of specially selected and paid miners through the shafts of the friendly Gould & Curry.

The pulse of the market rose and fell in normal sequence, but no word or action of the partners indicated that wealth to pale the treasure of the Incas was already in their hands and they continued to buy up Con Virginia and California whenever it appeared on the market. They called a meeting of the stockholders and increased the capital stock. They blocked the bonanza and knew they were among the richest men in the history of the world. Then they let their monstrous cat out of its bag.

Calling in Dan DeQuille, mining editor of the *Territorial Enterprise*, Fair assumed great indignation about the treatment he and his partners had received from the San Francisco papers, where they had long been regarded as fly-by-nights and common stock riggers.

"You tell them the truth, Dan," said Fair with a fine show of outraged virtue. "Go down there in Con Virginia and just tell them what you see."

DeQuille, a trusted and conservative mining reporter with years of Comstock experience behind him, went down in the mine, made his own measurements and computation and was so frightened by the result that he cut his estimate of the ore in sight by one half before publishing the result in his paper. Even thus halved, his story next morning announced there was visible in Con Virginia $116,748,000 worth of "finest chloride ore filled with streaks and bunches of the richest black silver sulphurettes." The implication, of course, was that California might be even richer since it lay adjacent and presumably shared the same ore mass.

Under the careful management of the four men who henceforth were to be known as the Kings of the Comstock, the valuation of the two mines on the San Francisco Exchange rose from $40,000 to $160,000,000. At the news of its discovery Bismarck ordered Germany off the silver standard. It made the dateline of Virginia City more important on news stories throughout the world than those of ancient capitals: London, Rome, Paris, or Madrid. It enriched many; it touched some with scandal, and its implications, fraudulently implemented by promoters, were eventually to cost speculators on the Pacific Coast nearly $400,000,000. These were the gulls who came to believe the entire Comstock was founded on riches as authentic as those of California and Con Virginia. But the four who had brought in the Big Bonanza and actually controlled its real and tangible riches became lords of creation, peers in the society of Crassus and Croesus, the Great Inca and the Indian Maharajahs, and eventually the Rockefellers and Mellons, the richest men of all time in the known world.

FLESHPOTS

It was one of the traditions of the American West that the de luxe devisings of life began to arrive in its mining camps almost as soon as the first prospectors had staked and recorded their claims. No sooner had he struck it really rich in the Matchless over in Colorado's Leadville than Horace W. Tabor, owner of everything in sight, told the proprietor of the Saddle Rock Cafe that he had better send to Delmonico's in New York for a chef worthy of his august clientele. In Central City the owner of the Teller House was in the habit of giving elaborate banquets with desserts representing his hostelry illuminated by cunning arrangements of gas lamps inside. In Nevada's later years Tonopah had an opera house and Goldfield an authentic French restaurant with Chicago prices-plus, almost before the first mine hoists were in operation. The California characters in Bret Harte spent an appreciable portion of their time eating Eastern oysters and drinking champagne out of magnums.

Virginia City was no exception to the rule of *grande lux*. Before there was so much as a board building in camp there was a reasonable choice of tent saloons and beer stoops literally excavated out of the side of Sun Mountain. The first brick building in town at the corner of A and Sutter streets was occupied by Wells Fargo & Co. and Charlie Sturm's Express Bar. Sturm had earlier occupied a tent saloon and had provided the flagon of whiskey with which "Old Virginny" had christened Virginia City, so who had a better right to the patronage of first citizens and pioneers? Penrod, Comstock & Co., for a time the first nabobs of the Comstock Lode, promised Sturm their exclusive patronage, a gesture calculated to guarantee him against any possibility of slack business. They also held their business meetings in the Express Bar.

A few years later, by the time Virginia City had become the howling wonder of the Western hemisphere and was being populated with its first crop of millionaires, the saloons were past all counting; and there was a choice of several dozen hotels of varying degrees of excellence and urbanity. Hennessy & Breen's, Pat Lynche's, Gentry & Crittenden's, Barnum's Restaurant and the tap room of Jacob Wimmer's Virginia Hotel were resorts of masculine fashion and communal foregathering ranking in splendor, convenience and resources, at least in the minds of their patrons, with the best Fifth Avenue had to offer.

But the true Periclean Age of Virginia and the Comstock was, of course, the splendid, silver seventies. Gone now were the wooden frame hotels and saloons. After having burned flat three separate times, the town had taken to building with brick. Gone, too, was the street fighting, stabbing, shooting, claim jumping and eventual lynching of the early years. Lawyers and, in consequence, some degree of law had come to Washoe and there were six precinct police stations in Virginia and Gold Hill with officers on constant duty. And culture and the resources of thunderous wealth had taken up their abode among the mine hoists.

Chief among their manifestations were the six story International Hotel and that ultimate citadel of voluptuous, nay, positively Babylonish luxuries, the Washoe Club. In these splendid precincts, in parlors draped in looped and fringed portiers, in corridors glittering with crystal chandeliers and in tap rooms graciously awash with the precious distillate of Bourbon County trod the nabobs in Prince Albert coats, silk top hats and wonderfully flowered waistcoats. Flunkies in livery responded to the summons of richly brocaded bellpulls. Crystal goblets and chalices from Vienna and the glass fac-

" 'TIS BUT A TENT WHERE TAKES HIS ONE
DAY'S REST"

The classic abode of Sultans in the "Rubaiyat" was plain indeed
compared to the abode of the nabobs and bonanza kings of the
Comstock. The International Hotel in its lifetime proclaimed
that very rich and very great was Virginia City. Its plush and
ormolu, crystal, gilt, marquetry and cloisonné all vanished in
one stupendous holocaust in the summer of 1914 but the story
of the hotel's magnificence lingers in Nevada as a fragrant sou-
venir of gaudy days and swaggering nights.

tories of Bohemia clinked and were elevated in salute. There was the smoke of dollar cigars everywhere.

The International Hotel was by no means only a local object of respectful admiration. Its state suites were counterparts of those in San Francisco's miraculous Palace Hotel, the finest the world had ever seen until then. From its upper floors the view extended eastward down Six Mile Canyon, past Sugar Loaf and almost to the reaches of the Sink of Carson itself. Its elevator, or "rising room" as it was known at the time, was the only one between Potter Palmer's expensive Chicago hostel and the Pacific Coast. Favored guests were permitted by the management to descend to its capacious cellars which spread far out beneath the sidewalks of C Street and draw their favorite spirits directly from the wood. A French maitre d'hotel had charge of its culinary destinies and shoals of Chinese house boys disposed instantly of every cigar butt that missed achieving one of the International's scores and scores of handsome and useful brass cuspidors.

The Washoe Club, located a block or two south of the International in C Street, was the scene of a stupendous dinner in honor of President Grant. Here, too, the nabobs, Flood, Fair, Mackay and O'Brien, played poker in uninterrupted sessions that lasted for days while the empty champagne bottles were carried away by the hamper and the gold double eagles passed across the table in foot-high stacks. It was at the Washoe that Mackay, by then one of the richest men in the entire world, told Dan de Quille that, since no amount he could conceivably win at cards could excite him, life seemed hardly worth the living.

Today the Washoe Club's furnishings, or some of the less perishable of them at least, are still visible in a C Street saloon that has assumed its name, but the last vestigial trace of the International Hotel disappeared when it went up in a blaze of seedy grandeur one summer night in 1914. Gone were its splendors of plush and ormolu, gilt and crystal, as indeed they had largely vanished before the end came. At the last even the elevator was a memory of departed splendors and guests were charged in reverse proportion to the number of steps they would have to climb to ascend to their rooms.

But the tradition of spacious times and of gaudy hurrah persists in Virginia City almost a century after its first flaming discovery. No historic shrine in the entire West can boast of more bars, oases, refreshment parlors and gaudy mantraps

THEN AND NOW IN C STREET

As late as 1912 when Virginia City was enjoying a final boom,
C Street was decorated with banners and bunting for the Fourth
of July and Bunny Nulty was elected "Queen Bunny" of the
festival. Two years later the International Hotel burned down
in a final blaze of grandeur and glory was gone from Virginia
City forever. The lower photograph shows C Street in mid-
twentieth century and the brick structure in the center, hidden
by the International in the earlier view, is the Carney Hotel
of today.

than still flourish along C Street. The past is recreated, vicariously, to be sure and with less violence than once obtained, but traces of its uninhibited manner are still discernible on Saturday night on the Comstock. The Bucket of Blood, the Delta, the Sawdust Corner and the Silver Stope, Reggie's Sky Deck, the Crystal Saloon and the Brass Rail all bear testimony to the vitality of their ancestral strain and forebears.

Should the delights of this galaxy of sluicements pall, there are others: Old 62, The Sazarac, The Smokery, the Virginia Club, The Golden Nugget and The Wonder Bar.

And on the hillside fringes of town at Taylor and Howard, a remarkable restaurant preserves the Comstock tradition of champagne in noble double magnums, of terrapin Maryland, venison chops and wonderful lamb from Minden, the lamb chop capital of the world, down in the valley. The Bonanza Inn, occupying the stateliest of surviving Comstock mansions of the bonanza era, is a gourmet's mecca in the grand manner famed throughout the West. There, under sixteen foot ceilings and amidst panels of matched circassian walnut, guests still dine in style and graciousness in the mansion that George Anson King built at a cost of $145,000 back in 1863 when the Comstock was young and lusty. If the ghost of John Mackay, on nights when the Nevada moon hangs over the Comstock, like all the moons of romance only bigger and brighter, stands musing on the landing of the great staircase in the house he once frequented, he would still recognize its sights and sounds, its candlelight and wine, its continuation, against all the long odds of time and chance, of the great way of life Virginia City once knew.

THE MUSE ABOVE THE MINESHAFTS

As spacious and romantic as any of the legends of the old West was its tradition of the theater. Often the muse came to the frontier hard upon the heels of the pioneers. Invariably it arrived there by the time crystal chandeliers and the presence of Wells Fargo & Co. indicated that the diggings were a proven camp and that things generally were here to stay. In an age when the Saratoga trunk and traveler's great cloak were as much the offstage properties of actors as dueling swords, Hamlet suits and other romantic fakements were behind the footlights, the American theater was an itinerant thing. It was not confined to New York, Boston and perhaps, greatly daring, Chicago as it is today. It rolled grandly up and down the continent aboard dusty Pullmans, stage coaches and river steamers, and billposters announcing the presence of Lola Montez and Lotta Crabtree were as familiar to Pickhandle Gulch and Okay Crossing as they were to Tremont Street or lower Broadway.

The West loved its opera houses and the players who, emerging from behind the red and gold velvet curtains of Victorian richness, brought Elsinore, Paris at midnight or the seacoast of Bohemia to the gold-rich, romance-hungry camps of Colorado, California and Nevada. Of all the old time playhouses whose boards knew the feet of Adah Isaacs Mencken and Salvinia the Younger, few survive today, Lost, at least to the Thespian mystery, are Haw Tabor's florid opera houses in Denver and snowy Leadville. Vanished from San Francisco are the Tivoli and the Grand Opera House, William Ralston's classic Old California Theater with the Free Public Library on its upper floors and the beautiful playhouse that was part of Lucky Baldwin's Hotel at Powell and Market. Gone from a score of Hangtowns, Eurekas and Bear Hills are the gaudy opera houses that once inflamed the civic bosom with pride and were regarded by jealous pastors as the veritable abode of Satin in their midst.

Only a few have survived the holocausts, floods and communal face liftings of the years: the famed and solid granite Opera House in Eureka Street of Colorado's Central City, the Bird Cage of lusty and robust repute in Tombstone's Tough Nut Street, and John Piper's once splendid Opera House on the top of the mineshafts of the Comstock.

Piper's as it exists today is Virginia City's third opera house and the second owned and managed by John Piper whose own Victorian mansion, built after the Great Fire of 1875, stands to this day at the southwest corner of A and Union Streets kitty-corner to the opera's stage door. Virginia's first theater was Maguire's New Opera House which opened in 1863 about the time the Washoe found itself securely enough established to go in for urban sophistication in a big way. It was a splendid thing, this first theater perched precariously and, as it turned out, briefly on the precipitous slope of Sun Mountain. There were, for one thing, carpets on the floor of aisles and gangways in contrast to the sawdust which had covered the boards of Virginia's places of public congregation to date. There was a magnificent curtain, its scene painted by a real art artist from Italy at reputedly fabulous expense, but actually in settlement of an overdue board bill at Jacob Wimmer's Virginia Hotel, depicting sunset at Lake Tahoe. A tasteful and cultivated scene in contrast to those in vogue behind the bars in C Street!

On opening night, when "Money" was billed for Virginia's first theatrical presentation, all the aristocracy of the Comstock turned out in its most stylish attire. The mine superintendents, the nabobs of Washoe, were present with their ladies on their arms and diamonds as big as robins' eggs in their starched shirt bosoms. The gamblers were there, conspicu-

WHERE HISTORY WAS MADE ON GASLIT NIGHTS

In the Comstock's gaudy heyday John Piper was king of its amusement world. He maintained and operated a succession of opera houses that were world famous. The third of these stands, somewhat precariously, to this day and is shown above while below is the interior where a stage box on every opening night was reserved for John Mackay and another for Adolph Sutro. Piper also maintained a series of saloons strategically situated hard by his theaters, thus assuring himself of the custom of the carriage trade both during and between the acts.

ously without ladies, but with diamonds somewhat bigger than those of the nabobs as compensation. Sandy Bowers and Eilley Orrum were not present at all. They were doing the Grand Tour of Europe and making life a trial for Charles Francis Adams, the American Ambassador to the Court of St. James, trying to get to have tea with Queen Victoria. Everyone agreed that, had Sandy been there, his diamonds would have been bigger than anyone's.

It was just after the orchestra had finished playing an overture and just before the house lights were dimmed that the shooting started. In an injudicious moment the management had seated two mortal enemies, Jack McNab and one Howard, in stage boxes on opposite sides of the auditorium but on the same level. Drawing a "Navy" revolver from under the tails of his broadcloth evening coat, McNab sighted across the plush mounted edge of his box and began firing. The elegantly printed program, composed and run in the job department of the *Territorial Enterprise,* leapt from Howard's suddenly palsied fingers. Another slug tore past his ear and shattered the crystals of an expensive wall fixture for lighting. Ladies screamed prettily. Gentlemen in other parts of the house arrived on the run from the bar, the billiard room and roulette parlor with an assortment of weapons, six-guns, champagne bottles and billiard cues. By this time MacNab's gun was empty and Howard, who it transpired was unarmed, was in full flight from the scene. Tranquility, or a reasonable facsimile thereof, was restored and the curtain, delayed a few minutes only, went up on "Money" with Walter Leman and Julia Dean Hayne in the leading roles.

Such was Virginia City's first, first night in the theater.

But Maguire's was not the only place of theatrical entertainment in Virginia City. Tent shows still flourished during the more clement months of the year and variety and the classics vied with each other for the patronage of miner, madame and millionaire. At one time there were five Shakespearean companies performing while six other troupes of mummers were presenting vaudeville, Tom shows, dog and pony acts and raree shows.

Washoe's taste in the theater was altogether catholic. It mattered little to customers whether the show at Maguire's was a performance of "Macbeth," a dogfight between fierce mastiffs, a brass band concert or "The Montgomery Queen's Great Show With the Only Female Somersault Rider in the World."

VIRGINIA CITY LOVED ALL SORTS OF SHOWS

Sometime in the nineties this dog and pony show came to Virginia City to fascinate the town's small fry with its gaily painted wagons and intelligent performing animals. Shown below is a poster depicting the Comstock's favorite, Adah Isaacs Menken, in the classic of the age, "Mazeppa," in which for climax she was carried from the stage bound to the back of a fiery stallion.

But among the more reputable players who came to Virginia City, riding up the Geiger Grade in the coaches of Wells Fargo & Co., and later aboard the cars of the Virginia & Truckee Railroad, were Adah Isaacs Mencken, Edwin Booth, John McCullough, Laurence Barrett, Clara Morris and Thomas Keene. "The Mencken" was a prime favorite of the miners because of her robust performance of "Mazeppa," a nineteenth century melodrama of Gothic proportions at the climax of which the heroine was carried off stage bound and approximately naked on the back of a coal black stallion. Wells Fargo provided a special express service to transport Mencken's trained equine performers throughout the West. Joe Jefferson was recalled again and again to Virginia City to play his classic "Rip Van Winkle," and "Davy Crockett" and "The Streets of New York" were tremendous attractions when billed with Frank Mayo in their leading roles. On one occasion, as a token of esteem, the miners presented Mencken with a bar of silver bullion worth $2,000. Wells Fargo's strongest stage had to be specially braced to ferry it down to the railroad at Reno!

In 1875 Maguire sold the Opera House to John Piper and within a year the conflagration of 1875 had wiped out his investment. With what had been minted gold, found after the ashes had cooled in a twisted mass of metal in the office safe, Piper at once rebuilt and speedily recouped his lost fortune. Again in 1883 fire destroyed the section of town where the Opera was located and again the indomitable Piper rebuilt in B Street where his theater stands to this day. David Belasco was at one time stage manager in these historic premises before moving on to greater things in New York and London.

Piper's hasn't heard a callboy going the rounds of its dressing rooms calling for curtain in many decades now, and Madame Helena Modjeska, General Tom Thumb and a young Otis Skinner are only wistful memories of departed grandeur. But the stage boxes sacred on opening nights to John Mackay and Adolph Sutro are still maintained by the management for visitors to see, tangible evidence of Virginia City's great days when gold pieces fell on the stage in a glittering shower for Adelina Patti and when the roars of approval of John Piper's uninhibited audiences wakened the midnight echoes in sleeping Six Mile Canyon. The show still goes on in the mind's eye of another generation.

THE DREAM OF ADOLPH SUTRO

Among the earliest comers to the Comstock in the white heat of its first fame in 1859 was Adolph Sutro, a Jewish cigar maker from San Francisco. A contemporary, in Washoe chronology at least, with such future nabobs as George Hearst and John Mackay, Sutro was possessed of an orderly and practical mind to which waste was anathema and the useless and unscientific dissipation of energy an abomination.

Upon arriving in Virginia City Sutro set out on a tour of inspection of the mines then in operation. Profit-taking started at the very roots of the sagebrush on the slopes of Sun Mountain, and such easy access to riches had banished all thought of anything even approximating scientific mining from the intelligence of the first miners. Ophir was little better than a cut in the hillside. Gould & Curry was being worked with Mexican peons under contract labor and no attempt was being made to reclaim any but the richest ores. The waste of less valuable ores was stupifying and they lay abandoned in the dumps to the value of hundreds of thousands of dollars.

Sutro's whole being was outraged. Here, he reflected, was a profile specifically created by nature for the easy, orderly and scientific working of its resources. The ore deposits lay on a hillside whence gravity, only slightly implemented by human ingenuity, would take them with an absolute minimum of waste labor down to the millsites along the Carson River. Obviously instead of sinking shafts straight down to follow the leads and fissures in their underground progress and then timbering up enormous chambers underground, the original shafts should be supplemented by a tunnel or tunnels dug in to meet them at right angles from lower down the hillside. Through this tunnel ore could be carried by gravity rather than by the expense of vast quantities of fuel to hoist it hundreds of feet vertically to the surface. Via the agency of a tunnel, too, it would be anywhere from five to six miles nearer Carson Water when the ore emerged to the light of day and all that distance would have been eliminated by a simple, gravity-activated underground tram instead of by costly teaming down the side of the mountain. The thing was so obvious as to be almost laughable.

But Sutro's tragedy was that to the easily satisfied miners of the Comstock's early years, his project *was* laughable. Why in heaven's name, they asked, should they be put to the trouble of digging a tunnel six miles long, even if such a project were practicable, which of course it wasn't, to ventilate shafts that were now practically open to the sky and carry out ore that already lay on the surface? The miners, who at this stage were recovering surface values, never foresaw that in a few weeks or months their shafts must sink to levels where their digging and maintenance would prove increasingly costly and hazardous and where their depth would easily justify a lateral tunnel dug in to meet them. Nor did they or even Sutro foresee the floods of boiling water which, at increased depths, could be removed only by the most powerful and costly surface pumps, yet easily could have been drained by the very tunnel Sutro proposed at but a fraction of the expense of tremendous pumping plants working night and 'day on a year around basis.

Five years after the Comstock's first excitements, its name was beginning to lose its power. The greedy manner in which the mines had been operating was having its effect and, more than anything else, their output was emperiled by water. Shortly thereafter it was to be entirely suspended. Perhaps the most dramatic example of the manner in which subterranean floods were able to defeat the shrewdest and most resolute superintendents was at Ophir. Ophir was the first to experi-

SUTRO'S MIGHTY PROJECT

Mule power pulled the little dummy cars of the Sutro tunnel and were largely responsible for its actual construction. The more obstinate of the creatures, during construction years, learned to come to a halt under the ventilators supplying fresh air in the earth's depths and had to be moved on by main force. Below is Adolph Sutro as he appeared when he became one of San Francisco's most beloved mayors.

ment with steam pumps in the hope of abating the seepage which, with every foot its shaft was sunk, became stronger and less controllable. A fifteen horsepower steam-activated pump was erected in San Francisco and installed while the Comstock held its breath. The pump functioned magnificently but it was soon apparent that, despite its satisfactory performance, it would require more and bigger pumps than existed anywhere to make an impression on the underground floods. Half of the mines along the Lode were closed and Virginia was in the midst of its first great panic.

Again Adolph Sutro came forward with his proposal of a tunnel to the Carson. His arguments now seemed more valid than they had before because, besides ventilating the mines and facilitating the economical, easy removal of ore, such a bore would perhaps drain off the waters that were plunging every shaft on Sun Mountain into borrasca. But there was powerful opposition to Sutro among the mine operators who were determined never to pay the two dollars a ton royalty that Sutro proposed to charge to defray the tunnel's cost of construction and operation. Sutro obtained articles of incorporation from the Nevada Legislature in 1865 but funds were not forthcoming from any source at all. Sutro pleaded with Congress in Washington for funds. In vain. He submitted prospectuses to Commodore Vanderbilt and William B. Astor in New York. In vain. He received encouragement in France but the approach of the Franco-Prussian War put an end to that hope.

It remained for one of the Comstock's periodic disasters to do more than all his own efforts had availed to promote Sutro's tunnel. In 1869 there occurred the terrible fire in the Yellow Jacket Mine which cost scores of lives and it became apparent to everyone that, had Sutro's tunnel been in operation as a subterranean fire escape, the holocaust need never have exacted so frightful a toll in life and treasure. With the united opinion of the Comstock miners behind him, Sutro scraped enough funds to begin work on his tunnel a short distance up the slope from Carson River in the fall of 1869.

Work on the tunnel was slow. Sutro had to meet a score of crises, most of them of a financial nature. The mines were booming again and a period of bonanza was earning unheard-of wealth for the operators of the mines while employment, too, was up and Sutro experienced difficulty in recruiting workmen for the construction of his project. The construction

WHEN LABOR'S KNIGHTHOOD WAS IN FLOWER

Adolph Sutro's destinies were largely shaped by the policies of the powerful Miners' Union, whose meeting hall stands to this day down the street from Piper's Opera. Until the time of the disastrous fire at Yellow Jacket the unions saw no virtue in his tunnel plan. When it was apparent that the existence of the tunnel would have made the catastrophe improbable the union men were Sutro men. His only trouble with his own miners was caused by their gregariousness. They hated working down Dayton way, far from the tumults and excitements of the Comstock towns. Mostly they hated being buried alone, but Sutro fixed that by originating a union graveyard for tunnel casualties and after that had no trouble with his workers.

of the Virginia & Truckee Railroad was also a threat since its completion materially cut the cost of freighting ore down to the mills along Carson River, a boon which Sutro had planned to confer on the Comstock himself.

But, despite all opposition of man and nature, Sutro by May of 1878 was working at a depth of 2,000 feet under Virginia City and only 640 feet from the nearest operations of the Lode. Sutro was personally peddling small blocks of tunnel stock to anyone he could interest but relief was closer at hand than he had dared to imagine. At the 2,000 foot level all the mines of the Comstock were again encountering floods of hot water and no pumps on earth could avail to pump these steaming tides from such depths. Four of the biggest mines, Hale & Norcross, Best & Belcher, Savage and Crown Point suddenly capitulated and agreed to pay Sutro his two dollars royalty if he could finish his tunnel before they were irrevocably ruined. Only the mines producing the Big Bonanza, the California and Consolidated Virginia, held out.

On July 8 Sutro himself fired the final charge of dynamite which demolished the last underground barrier between his tunnel heading and the Savage shaft and, stripped to the waist and sweat-grimed as any laborer, stepped through the breach. After thirteen years of continued battle he had triumphed over his enemies in the ranks of the mine operators and over the implacable hostility of the forces of nature deep underground in the approaches to Sun Mountain.

Ironically the great Sutro tunnel was completed at the precise moment when the fortunes of the Comstock and Virginia City started the last great decline from which they never recovered. But there were still many years of unspectacular activity ahead on Sun Mountain and the tunnel, which had cost more than $5,000,000, paid off handsomely and remained in useful operation until the forties of the present century when deep mining on the Comstock was entirely suspended. In one year it drained more than 2,000,000,000 gallons through its laterals and connecting passages.

Sutro sold out his interest in the property at a profit and left Nevada to become one of San Francisco's most respected public citizens and a benefactor of many good causes, while the tunnel of which he dreamed, although of scant moment by comparison to the titanic feats of engineering which the twentieth century was to evoke, will remain for all time an integral part of the Comstock story.

NABOBS IN BROADCLOTH

The Comstock was to produce a multitude of great names, some of them of world consequence, others that blazed brightly on a national scale. There was Adolph Sutro, the tunnel builder who was to become one of the most celebrated of San Francisco's mayors and whose name adorns many municipal institutions surviving to this day. There was George Hearst who was to become a California senator in Washington and whose fortune was one day to finance the most important chain of newspapers and magazines ever to be published in the United States. There was Mark Twain who served his literary apprenticeship on the staff of the *Territorial Enterprise* and David Belasco who, as a youth, was stage manager at Piper's Opera. And there was Henry B. Yerington, one of the greatest of Western railroad operators, and Wells Drury, a journalist in the spacious tradition of the nineteenth century newspaper world.

But the names that most fascinated their own generation were those of the Silver Kings, the Lords of Creation, the Big Four of the Comstock Lode, Flood, Fair, Mackay and O'Brien and the other princely seekers and finders of fortune who came to Virginia City with an Ames shovel over their shoulders and departed for palaces on Nob Hill or in the Rue Tilsit.

One of the most arrestingly picturesque of them was William M. Stewart, graduate of Yale Law School, a graduate, too, of the Mother Lode camps of the early fifties and later a Nevada senator and greatest expert on mining litigation in the West. Stewart, who was accustomed to try cases involving dangerous characters fully armed with a brace of Navy Colts under the skirts of his frock coat, was the first real law on the Comstock. His interpretation of justice was invariably in favor of whoever might have retained him, but his courage and tenacity were monumental in a generation when both of these qualities were in great requisition. Stewart went on to bigger things in Washington and lived a long and wealthy life in the later Nevada bonanzas, but until his dying day he was a bad man to cross, and the world, or most of it, knew that under his patriarchal beard there was apt to be a shoulder holster and that Stewart's law was not to be held lightly.

Another of the nabobs of note was John Percival Jones, hero of the great Crown Point fire at the time he was superintendent. Jones also became a Nevada senator and was the driving force behind the now almost forgotten Panamint excitement across the California line in the Death Valley region. Historians remember Panamint as one of the most alluring, deceptive and geographically improbable bonanzas high in the Panamint Mountains where, at Jones' command, an entire civilization once flourished briefly, sold a blizzard of worthless securities and finally disappeared forever when a cloudburst destroyed the diggings at Panamint City almost without a trace.

Graduates of the Virginia City school of experience enlivened the known world for two full generations.

But hard head and broad shoulder above all the silk hatted rout of Comstock millionaires, king of the bonanza kings and a favorite of fortune whose name was destined to rank with those of Morgans, Rockefellers, Vanderbilts, Mellons and Whitneys, John Mackay was one of the very few, who, when greatness claimed him, never forgot its origins and never altogether deserted the Comstock.

Mackay was one of those who toiled up Six Mile with an Ames shovel on his shoulder. Among the first arrivals from the abandoned riffles and Long Toms of the California Sierra,

PICNICS AND PARADES

On a Sunday afternoon in the eighties this group of picnickers gathered at the Bowers Mansion in Washoe Meadows, a study of style in the age of chatelaine watches, Ascot ties and curly brimmed bowler hats. Below is a Fourth of July parade of the same period in B Street, locally known as "Bonanza Avenue," with the residents of the stylish mansions out on their front steps in fashionable attire to cheer the marchers.

MONUMENTS TO THE COMSTOCK WEALTH

Jim Flood, the former San Francisco saloon proprietor, suffered from no inhibitions when it came to spending his great Comstock wealth. Above is the brownstone mansion which he erected on Nob Hill and which today houses the Pacific Union Club, while below is the palatial country home at Menlo Park, a miracle of turrets, gables and gingerbread which was known to Californians of its day as "Flood's Wedding Cake."

HOW JIM FAIR SPENT HIS MONEY

Because of his evasive business ethics, James G. Fair was known in his latter years as "Slippery Jim" but there was never any doubt about his ability as a hard-rock mining man. Above is his B Street home in Virginia City and below his Pine Street mansion in San Francisco where the wedding in 1890 of Tessie Fair and Herman Oelrichs was a social dazzlement of national importance and vast and wealthy implications.

he went to work in the first shallow diggings on the slopes of
Sun Mountain and within two decades was to be known
throughout the civilized world as the quintessential American
success story. It was his good fortune and that of his associates, more often than not backed by resources of intelligence and determination not always credited in the record,
that made the Comstock what Oscar Lewis has called "the
nation's most satisfactory wishing well."

Like Adolph Sutro, Mackay found the early operations on
the Comstock so wasteful and unsophisticated as to be positively repellent, but he was to live to see the management in
his own mines regarded by experts as the pinnacle of deep
mining technique and the most economical of his generation.

After holding down a variety of jobs in the mines which by
this time were appearing along the Lode in florid abundance
and observing shrewdly into the conduct, or more often mis-
conduct of their fortunes, Mackay went to work in the Kentuck Mine, taking his pay not in cash to be converted into
Saturday night whiskey and Sunday remorse, but in shares in
the company. In 1863 the owners of the Kentuck sought to
incorporate but found they were powerless to do so without
possession of a number of "feet" (all shares were calculated
not in dollars but in running footage of the property) owned
by one of the original discoverers. The shareholder was
reported to be among the Confederate armies fighting in the
campaigns of western Tennessee and a fat bonus was posted
for the recovery of his proxy.

That was enough for Mackay. The Comstock knew him not
for four long months although he was reported to have been
a passenger on one of Ben Holladay's overland stages heading
for the Mississippi. When he reappeared it was with the miss-
ing block of feet and a bill of sale to show his ownership.
Mackay never revealed how he secured them but the legend
insists he dogged his man into the front lines before Chatta-
nooga and wrangled over the price while Parrott rifles
boomed and minié balls ripped overhead. Now Kentuck
could be incorporated and Mackay was for the first time an
active capitalist on the basis of his share in the property.

Kentuck turned out to be a bonanza of modest proportions
— over a period of years it produced about $5,000,000 — but
his share was enough to put behind Mackay forever his days
as a $4 pick-and-shovel man or later $6 as timber worker.
Once in his Mother Lode days Mackay had remarked that

when he made $200,000 he was going to retire and that the man who wanted more was a fool, but success was now in his veins and with the profits from Kentuck he joined forces with James G. Fair, an alliance which was eventually to lead to the Big Bonanza and the emergence of the kings of the Comstock.

The story of the Big Bonanza is told in more detail elsewhere in this volume, but its discovery made Mackay and his associates, Fair, Flood and O'Brien, the one-time San Francisco saloon proprietors, into men of incredible consequence. Of the four, Mackay proved the most capable of bearing the almost intolerable burden of fantastic wealth.

Mackay was married in Virginia City in the parlor of Slippery Jim Fair's cottage to Marie Bryant, widow of a Downieville surgeon and daughter of Daniel Hungerford, the town barber, in 1866. It was the beginning of a saga of social dazzlements and unparalleled displays of wealth which were to astound even blasé Paris and London in a blasé age, and whose echoes were reawakened in the world press of the 1920's when Mackay's granddaughter Ellen was married to Irving Berlin over the aristocratic protest of the existing Mackay family. To this day Mrs. Berlin is a frequent pilgrim to the Comstock to revisit the scene of her mighty grandfather's mightiest triumphs.

Mrs. Mackay, now armed with formidable financial resources and a naïve determination to display them, removed herself permanently from the United States and set out to conquer formal society in the Old World while Mackay himself, glad to be quit of frivolities, footed her bills on condition that he should be omitted from her campaigns and conquests.

Not without a sense of the ridiculous, Mackay made it a point, upon the occasion of his infrequent visits to his wife's palaces in Paris and London, to affect the uncouth American millionaire as foreigners expected him. He resolutely refused to learn French, thereby forcing his dinner partners to converse in English to their notable disadvantage. Instead of the rare clarets and noble champagnes served by Mrs. Mackay's wine stewards and major-domos he insisted on a shot of straight Bourbon with the pheasant. He took a mildly malicious pleasure in recalling his boyhood days in Dublin and insisted that his family's pig shared the parlor in the best shanty Irish tradition. He was, in a word, a trial while among the dignitaries, so that his wife was glad to see him depart as soon as possible for San Francisco or his beloved Comstock. In actuality Mackay was an extremely well read, urbane and polished man of the world in which he lived.

The whole tally of Mackay's charities will never be known to anyone. Almost in their entirety, and that was in the millions, they were contributed to causes he considered worthy on condition that they should be absolutely anonymous. Such institutional benevolences as the Church of St. Mary's in the Mountains in Virginia City and the Mackay School of Mines at Reno could not well be hidden, but there were quite literally loans to oldtime friends on the Comstock and donations to worthy beneficiaries running into the millions. It was because of this patrician disregard for expenditures in what he considered to be commendable channels that at Mackay's death in 1902 his business manager was able to tell the reporters: "I don't suppose he knew within twenty millions what he was worth."

Mackay was the greatest example of the Comstock's incalculable power for good. The wealth he wrested from the California and Con Virginia mines was translated into continental railroads and trans-Atlantic cables, telegraph systems, sugar refineries, copper mills and productive real estate. Perhaps, indeed, probably he derived pleasure from the power and authority his great fortune gave him, but the Comstock nearly half a century after his death, remembers him for a disillusioned remark he made one night in the Washoe Club at a time when his income was close to a million dollars a year, a sum the equivalent in purchasing power of four or five times as much today.

"I don't care whether I win or lose," he told Dan de Quille. "And when you can't enjoy winning at poker, there's no fun left in anything."

Perhaps that will serve as John Mackay's epitaph until a better one comes along.

SUNSET OVER THE SIERRA

For nine decades now the Comstock has been an integral part of the legend of the American West. For nearly half of this period it was a producer of wealth in one of the most tangible of its many forms and for the other half of its inhabited and exploited existence it has been a romantic fragment of the national history of the land. It has inspired a wealth of lore and literature to the extent of a very considerable bibliography of serious books and has served as a background for a good deal of fiction which never surpassed the actual recorded fact. It has occupied space in the American consciousness out of all proportion to its geographic size or population. Even today it advertises itself to the tourist trade as "the livest ghost town in the world" and there is a surprising degree of truth in this brash boast.

The shrinking violet could never with any plausibility be selected as the official flower of the State of Nevada.

Where the bonanza kings left off on the Comstock the literary lions took over. The legend of the Lode is as completely irresistible to writers as ever the original "blue stuff' was to James Finney or Pat McLaughlan and its various aspects have engaged such first rate men of letter as Oscar Lewis, Eliot Lord, Samuel Bowles, Sam Davis and Wells Drury. Even the Virginia & Truckee Railroad is the subject of a very respectable bibliography and the learned treatises on the mining of Comstock are beyond accurate counting.

Surprisingly enough, however, the Carson River, or Carson Water as it is known in the stately old phrase, has never come in for its share of romantic treatment although it is one of the most romantic little rivers in the world. Probably the fact that it is not navigable and that no vast civilizations were ever borne upon its tides has led to this neglect, but Carson Water made possible a great and spectacular productivity as ever floated upon the Mystic, the Ohio or the Colorado. Without it the milling of Comstock ores would have been impossible by any process known to the nineteenth century and the necessity for transporting ore over vast distances to mills in other parts of the land would have been incalculably costly.

The Carson is well worth the attention of a curious and enquiring generation. A remote and lonely stream, it rises in the foothills of the High Sierra, flows briefly north and east to its appointments with destiny and disappears ingloriously into the Sink of Carson without ever knowing the sea which is the objective of almost all respectable and conventional rivers. In spring it is a rushing torrent that inundates vast meadows and downlands around Minden and Gardnerville. By midsummer it is a placid meander whose pools and backwater entice the judicious picnicker and occasional crayfisherman in the neighborhood of Empire and Dayton. In winter it is a gelid streamlet impervious alike to the devisings of mankind or the zephyrs of Washoe. Always it is a lonely and often a beautiful little river winding its way to a lonely and geologically improbable end.

But once it was a river of mighty consequence. When its stamping mills and reducing plants stretched for miles above Carson City and Empire its waters were carefully husbanded and used over and over again by the successive mills along its banks. Its existence was the basic fact that lay behind the construction of the railroad. Its presence made possible all the operations of the far-reaching and consequential Comstock. It was a river of humble origins and appearance but of weighty importance in the affairs of men. The locomotives of the V & T prowled beside the river on a vast network of spurs and sidings, but today little remains save an occasional cement foundation or vast and ruined machinery sprawling like the skeletons of prehistoric monsters in a wilderness of vines and scrub trees.

There are other pleasant places to explore around the Comstock. Few persons other than native Nevadans know that the Geiger Grade on which they approach Virginia City from the main highway at Steamboat Springs is not the original Geiger but a much later and vastly safer trail. The old original Geiger over which the stages of Wells Fargo toiled with their treasure until the coming of the railroad is still available to traffic a few thousand feet from the surfaced grade and is an infinitely more picturesque and exciting drive.

Then there is Six Mile Canyon which leads by a precipitous and craggy route down to Sutro past the ruins of a score of once tremendous and vibrant reducing plants and stamp mills. As lately as 1904 the great Butters reducing plant was built to employ 300 workers in Six Mile, but all that remains today is a heap of ruined masonry, mute testimonial to unjustified optimism. And there are agreeable and exploratory drives to be made to Jumbo and Como, but they are not strictly speaking a part of the Comstock.

The years of the Second World War were bleak ones for the Comstock. The V & T had misguidedly torn up its tracks between Carson and Virginia and the rationing of gasoline eliminated the tourist trade almost in its entirety. For lack of repairs whole blocks of buildings in the lower town collapsed and disappeared, their structural economy having been sawed up into firewood. Mining was prohibited by the government and without mining or tourists and with a diminishing supply of liquor Virginia City was in a bad case.

Now, however, the Comstock is enjoying the sort of boom it dreamed of during the dark days. Interest in its historic aspects becomes greater with each passing year and the presence of a small but distinguished literary colony adds impressively to the town's prestige. Its literary lights include Roger Butterfield, author of "The American Past"; Duncan Emrich, assistant librarian of Congress for American folklore; Walter van Tilburg Clark, whose "Oxbow Incident" and "Track of the Cat" have been national best sellers; and Irene Bruce, a lady poetess in the best bohemian tradition of the craft. If this were not distinction enough for a community of 400 persons, Doctor Emrich's wife is author of a number of well known juvenile books and Katharine Hillyer and Katherine

Here Mrs. Emmy Wood, owner of the famed Flying "M E" Ranch in Washoe Meadows, listens to an after dinner story at Bonanza Inn as told by Vail Pittman, Governor of Nevada. Below, Sheldon Pennoyer, celebrated painter of Comstock subjects and Tahoe resident, chats with Mrs. Vail Pittman and the Earl of Cowley, owner of a showplace ranch in Lakeview near Carson City. The Earl, who is also Lord Wellesley, heir to the title of a great English family, prefers in Nevada to be known simply as Mr. Wellesley.

In the upper picture four Comstock literary notables line up for a buffet lunch on "Authors' Day." They are, left to right, Mrs. Duncan Emrich, Dr. Duncan Emrich, Assistant Librarian of Congress; Walter van Tilburg Clark, author of "The Track of the Cat"; and Irene Bruce, lady poet of the Comstock. Below, Halvor Smedsrud, host of the Bonanza Inn, pours wine for Roger Butterfield, author of "The American Past," and Mrs. Ruth Lusch, publicist for Bonanza Air Lines, a Nevada transport service.

Best are magazine writers of national fame. The Reno Chamber of Commerce, which takes a proprietary interest in all the adjacent countryside, never misses an opportunity to point with pride to Nevada's mining town culture.

A number of the town's most famous structures were destroyed in the Great Fire of 1875 and most of its architecture today dates from that and succeeding years. Most notable of the post-conflagration landmarks is the Roman Catholic Church of St. Mary's of the Mountains whose original was among the losses that dark day in October '75. John Mackay was frantically engaged with his own workmen in saving the lower workings of his Consolidated Virginia Mine when news was brought to him that St. Mary's was gone. In the gloom and excitement of the moment Mackay promised to "rebuild twenty churches" if his mine was saved and he later handsomely lived up to his promise, although a single edifice seemed sufficient for the religious needs of the community.

The deep mining of precious metals has entirely disappeared from Virginia City itself, but across "The Divide" in Gold Hill a few deep mines are still in operation and their hoists can be seen actively disgorging ore which is nowadays removed in thundering motor trucks. But by far the most important operations in gold and silver are being conducted in Gold Hill and Silver City through the agency of open pit or "strip" mines in which surface values are recovered with the aid of modern earth moving machinery and reduced by the cyanide process at one of the several still active reducing mills which line the old road up to Grinder's Bend just south of The Divide. Perhaps "old road" isn't entirely correct, for in 1949 so profitable were the operations in the Donovan strip mine adjacent to the original highway that Bill Donovan was able to persuade the Storey County authorities to let him cart its entire grade for more than a mile off to his mill after he had removed and rebuilt the highway complete with its power and communications installation a thousand yards away from its original site.

The last deep mining in Virginia City was done in Consolidated Virginia in 1927. The very lowest levels below the Sutro Tunnel were closed in 1922.

Surface mining today includes the operations of the Dayton Consolidated Mines Co., working through the New York shaft; Consolidated Chollar Gould & Savage Mining Co., working in Overman Mine; the Bill Donovan's Double Kings

THE GLORY IS DEPARTED FROM GOLD HILL

When the upper photograph was taken in the seventies Gold Hill was a rich mining community second in productivity on the Comstock to Virginia City alone. Today, as shown below, its shafts and hoisting works are dust and its population is a mere handful where once thousands lived and toiled and grew wealthy.

OLD HOUSES IN THE SUN

These old houses in the lower town dreaming away the autumn
of their years are veterans of the age of Virginia City's proudest
destinies. The nabob's mansion once knew the tread of John
Mackay, of Adolph Sutro, and the old bearded kings of Nevada's
argentine destinies. The dusty roadway was once rutted with
the carriages of mine superintendents and San Francisco arch-
millionaires in silk hats and skirted frock coats. Time and the
elements, which deal gently with few things on the Comstock,
have spared them for a later generation to marvel at the life
and times of which they are the benevolent and aged symbols.

Mine working in Silver Hill; and the Central Comstock Mining Co., working tailings in Virginia City. Dayton Consolidated's Mine is in Gold Hill, its mill in Silver City. Consolidated Chollar's mine and mill are both in Gold Hill and the Donovans' mill is in Silver City and their mine in Gold Hill.

Mills use either the counter current cyanide process or a combination flotation and cyanide process and handle from 150 tons to 500 tons a day. Consolidated Chollar mills about 500 tons and Central Comstock 300 tons daily. The Donovans ship approximately 3,500 ounces of silver and 350 ounces of gold per month to the mint in San Francisco or Washington in bullion bars containing both metals which are separated at the mint.

There is still, too, a stamp mill in operation not ten feet from the Silver City-Gold Hill highway, and midnight motorists, unaware of its existence and unfamiliar with its characteristic noisy rigadoon, are often startled and mystified when they first encounter the symphony of its thundering stamps which has been for so many decades the true music of the Comstock.

Amateurs of the American past and of the old West see in Virginia City one of the few remaining examples of the hell and high waters days of the frontier and the individualist. There are vestigial remnants of the nineteenth century elsewhere in the land, notably Central City and Leadville in Colorado; Tombstone, Arizona; Columbia in the Mother Lode; and the other Virginia City, that one in Montana. None of these however seem to retain the ancient flavor of character at once raffish and sophisticated that abides in the Comstock. The great days may be irrevocably gone but those which have followed them in Nevada are still sufficiently spacious to serve as a reminder of a notable manner of life patterned in the American way.

SUPPLEMENTARY READING ON THE COMSTOCK LEGEND

The Big Bonanza, Dan De Quille

An Editor on the Comstock Lode, Wells Drury

Bonanza Railroads, Gilbert Kneiss

Silver Kings, Oscar Lewis

Mark Twain in Nevada, Effie Mona Mack

The Saga of the Comstock Lode, George D. Lyman

Eilley Orrum, Queen of the Comstock, Swift Paine

Roughing It, Samuel L. Clemens

Nevada, A Guide to the Silver State, Works Progress Administration

Via Western Express and Stagecoach, Oscar O. Winther

Nevada's Metal and Mineral Production, Nevada State Bureau of Mines

Nevada, Colorado and Wyoming, Hubert Howe Bancroft

History of Nevada, Sam P. Davis

Mark Twain's America, Bernard de Voto

The Big Bonanza, C. B. Glasscock

Comstock Mining and Miners, Eliot Lord

Virginia & Truckee, Lucius Beebe and Charles Clegg

U.S. West, The Saga of Wells Fargo, Lucius Beebe and Charles Clegg

A HARDY BOOK